JOHN D. ROCKEFELLER ON MAKING MONEY

JOHN D. ROCKEFELLER ON MAKING MONEY

Advice and Words of Wisdom on Building and Sharing Wealth

JOHN D. ROCKEFELLER

Skyhorse Publishing

Note: Spelling has been lightly edited to conform to modern standards of American English

Copyright © 2015 by Skyhorse Publishing, Inc.

Skyhorse Publishing books may be purchased in bulk at special discounts for sales promotion, corporate gifts, fund-raising, or educational purposes. Special editions can also be created to specifications. For details, contact the Special Sales Department, Skyhorse Publishing, 307 West 36th Street, 11th Floor, New York, NY 10018 or info@skyhorsepublishing.com.

Skyhorse® and Skyhorse Publishing® are registered trademarks of Skyhorse Publishing, Inc.®, a Delaware corporation.

Visit our website at www.skyhorsepublishing.com.

10 9 8 7 6

Library of Congress Cataloging-in-Publication Data is available on file.

Cover design by Jane Sheppard

Print ISBN: 978-1-63220-623-7
Ebook ISBN: 978-1-63220-737-1

Printed in the United States of America

CONTENTS

JOHN D. ROCKEFELLER ON MAKING MONEY

CHAPTER 1

BIG BUSINESS IN AMERICA

Competition is a sin.

I would rather earn one percent off one hundred people's efforts than one hundred percent of my own efforts.

❧

The day of individual competition in large affairs is past and gone—you might just as well argue that we should go back to hand labor and throw away our efficient machines—and the sober good sense of the people will accept this fact when they have studied and tried it out.

❧

In all times past, the weak man in the competition dropped out and was lost sight of. These men for years were importuned to join hands with those who were stronger and ready to pull them out from their embarrassments and fit them in to be useful in the administration of the Standard Oil Company so far as they had integrity, intelligence, enterprise and industry to warrant the expectation that they could be stones in the foundation of the great structure, the likes of which the world had never seen.

It is too late to argue about advantages of industrial combinations. They are a necessity. And if Americans are to have the privilege of extending their business in all the states of the Union, and into foreign countries as well, they are a necessity on a large scale, and require the agency of more than one corporation.

The dangers are that the power conferred by combination may be abused, that combinations may be formed for speculation in stocks rather than for conducting business, and that for this purpose prices may be temporarily raised instead of being lowered.

The Standard Oil Company has been one of the greatest, if not the greatest, of upbuilders we ever had in this country— or in any country. All of which has inured to the benefit of the towns and cities the country over; not only in our country but the world over. And that is a very pleasant reflection now as I look back. I knew it at the time, though I realize it more keenly now.

The country's resources have not been cut down nor injured by financial distrust. A gradual recovery will only tend to make the future all the more secure, and patience is a virtue in business affairs as in other things.

We had vision, saw the vast possibilities of the oil industry, stood at the center of it, and brought our knowledge and imagination and business experience to bear in a dozen—twenty, thirty—directions. There was no branch of the business in which we did not make money.

It will be said: "Here was a force that reorganized business, and everything else followed it—all business, even the government itself, which legislated against it."

Beyond question there is a suspicion of corporations. There may be reason for such suspicion very often; for a corporation may be moral or immoral, just as a man may be moral or the reverse; but it is folly to condemn all corporations because some are bad, or even to be unduly suspicious of all, because some are bad. But the corporation in form and character has come to stay— that is a thing that may be depended upon.

◆

I don't want a nation of thinkers; I want a nation of workers.

◆

Don't blame the marketing department. The buck stops with the chief executive.

◆

Good management consists of showing average people how to do the work of superior people.

᭡᭡

The growth of a large business is merely a survival of the fittest ... The American Beauty rose can be produced in the splendor and fragrance which bring cheer to its beholder only by sacrificing the early buds which grow up around it. This is not an evil tendency in business. It is merely the working-out of a law of nature and a law of God.

᭡᭡

The day of combination is here to stay. Individualism has gone, never to return.

᭡᭡

Probably the greatest single obstacle to the progress and happiness of the American people lies in the willingness of so many men to invest their time and money in multiplying competitive industries instead of opening up new fields, and putting their money into lines of industry and development that are needed.

❦

When a man has accumulated a sum of money, accumulated it within the law, the government has no right to share in its earnings.

❦

I never go into an enterprise unless I feel sure it is coming out all right. For instance, a promising scheme may be proposed to me. It may not altogether satisfy and is rejected.

❦

The great business interests will, I hope, so comport themselves that foreign capital will consider it a desirable thing to hold shares in American companies. It is for Americans to see that foreign investors are well and honestly treated, so that they will never regret purchases of our securities.

None of us ever dreamed of the magnitude of what proved to be the later expansion. We did our day's work as we met it, looking forward to what we could see in the distance and keeping well up to our opportunities, but laying our foundations firmly.

I wanted able men with me. I tried to make friends with these men. I admitted their ability and the value of their enterprise. I worked to convince them that it would be better for both to cooperate . . . and if I had not succeeded in getting their friendship the whole plan of the Standard Oil Company would have fallen to the ground. I admit I tried to attract only the able men; and I have

always had as little as possible to do with
dull business men.

It is not always the easiest of tasks to
induce strong, forceful men to agree.

Combination is necessary and its abuses
can be minimized; otherwise our legislators
must acknowledge their incapacity to
deal with the most important instrument
of industry. Hitherto most legislative
attempts have been not to control but to
destroy; hence their futility.

In working with so many partners, the
conservative ones are apt to be in the majority,
and this is no doubt a desirable thing when
the mere momentum of a large concern is

certain to carry it forward. The men who have been very successful are correspondingly conservative, since they have much to lose in case of disaster. But fortunately there are also the aggressive and more daring ones, and they are usually the youngest in the company, perhaps few in number, but impetuous and convincing. They want to accomplish things and to move quickly, and they don't mind any amount of work or responsibility.

If we limit opportunity we will have to put the brakes on our national development. Will the individual strive for success if he knows the hard-won prize is to be snatched from him at last by his government? We must build up, build up for years to come.

Is it common sense to tell our young men on whom the future depends that they can hope for no other reward for carrying our commercial flag forward than frenzied attacks at home? And all the handicaps their government can pile on their business to satisfy the violent prejudice against them? Take the attack we made upon our own packing business, for example. I know none of the men in the beef trade. I never dealt with them . . . But it is safe to assume from the proportions of their industry that they are sound business men. And it is safe to assume too that no business could have been built to such proportions on such false principles or by such unsound methods as they are charged with. We are too young a nation for this tearing down.

⚬✎⚬

That is [the Standard Oil Company's] mission, to light the world with the cheapest and best.

Europe is a nice place, but I love my country best. Yes, all the hard things that my countrymen say of me can never be cruel enough to offset my love of country and home.

We are leading an awful fast life in this country . . . It's rush, rush, rush all the time.

I had a peculiar training in my home. It seemed to be a business training from the beginning.

I shall never forget how hungry I was in those days. I ran up and down the tops of freight cars . . . I hurried up the boys.

To my mind there is something unfortunate in being born in the city. You have not had the struggles in the city that we have had who were reared in the country. Don't you notice how the men from the country keep crowding you out here—you who have wealthy fathers? These young men from the country are turning things around and are taking your city. We men from the country are willing to do more work. We were prepared by our experience to do hard work.

CHAPTER 2

FACING CRITICISM

. . . it has always been the policy of the Standard to keep silent under attack and let our acts speak for themselves.

⌘

You can abuse me, you can strike me, if you will only let me have my own way.

A great number of scientific men every year give up everything to arrive at some helpful contribution to the sum of human knowledge, and I have sometimes thought that good people who lightly and freely criticize their actions scarcely realize just what such criticism means. It is one thing to stand on the comfortable ground of placid inaction and put forth words of cynical wisdom, and another to plunge into the work itself and through strenuous experience earn the right to express strong conclusions.

I am not afraid of reporters publishing what I say but what I do not say.

There has been nothing in my life that will not bear the utmost scrutiny. Is it not patent that I have been made into a sort of frightful ogre to slay, which has become a favorite resource of men seeking public favor? It is not from the body of the people whence I sprang that these denunciations come, but from the self-seekers who would be leaders. What advantages had I that every other poor boy did not possess? No one could have begun life with less than I had. Does any fair man accuse me of grinding him down?

⌒∞⌒

I am not one who wears his heart on his sleeve, and I cannot bring myself to make fit answer to these repeated slanders. But it is a fact that all of this criticism comes from, or is inspired by, men who have been my business competitors—men who would have bested me if I had not bested them—and from public officials seeking favor, agitators, and demagogues.

A man so busy cannot be always right. We are all bound to make mistakes at times.

I never despair. Sometimes things that are said of me are cruel and they hurt, but I am never a pessimist. I believe in man and the brotherhood of man, and I am confident that everything will come out for the good of all in the end.

Criticism which is deliberate, sober, and fair is always valuable and it should be welcomed by all who desire progress. I have had at least my full share of adverse criticism, but I can truly say that it has not embittered me, nor left me with any harsh feeling against a living soul. Nor do I wish to be critical of those whose conscientious judgment, frankly expressed, differs from my own. No matter how noisy the pessimists may be, we know that the world is getting better steadily and rapidly, and that is a good thing to remember in our moments of depression or humiliation.

CHAPTER 3

MAN AND MONEY

I know of nothing more despicable and pathetic than a man who devotes all the hours of the waking day to the making of money for money's sake.

The way to make money is to buy when blood is running in the streets.

A man of business may often most properly consider that he does his share in building up a property which gives steady work for few or many people; and his contribution consists in giving to his employees good working conditions, new opportunities, and a strong stimulus to good work. Just so long as he has the welfare of his employees in his mind and follows his convictions, no one can help honoring such a man. It would be the narrowest sort of view to take, and I think the meanest, to consider that good works consist chiefly in the outright giving of money.

If your only goal is to become rich, you will never achieve it.

I have ways of making money you know nothing about.

A man's wealth must be determined by the relation of his desires and expenditures to his income. If he feels rich on ten dollars, and has everything else he desires, he really is rich.

Do you know what would hurt grandfather a great deal? To know that any of you boys should become wasteful, extravagant, careless with his money.

The impression was gaining ground with me that it was a good thing to let the money be my slave and not make myself a slave to money.

I had no ambition to make a fortune. Mere money making has never been my goal. I saw a marvelous future for our country, and I wanted to participate in the work of making our country great. I had an ambition to build.

You will find [money] the best of friends—if not the best friend—you have.

I know of some people, especially young men, who find it very difficult to keep a little money in their pocketbooks. I learned to keep the money, and, as we had a way of saying, "it didn't burn a hole in my pocket." I was taught that it was the thing to do to keep the money and to take care of it.

I think money is a good thing to have if we know how to use it properly. I think it is very harmful to many people because they do not know how to use it properly.

To my father I owe a great debt in that he himself trained me to practical ways.

He was engaged in different enterprises; he used to tell me about these things, explaining their significance; and he taught me the principles and methods of business. From early boyhood I kept a little book which I remember I called Ledger A—and this little volume is still preserved—containing my receipts and expenditures as well as an account of the small sums that I was taught to give away regularly.

Every right implies a responsibility; every opportunity, an obligation; every possession, a duty.

I spoke just now of the struggle for success. What is success? Is it money? Some of you have all the money you need to provide for your wants. Who is the poorest man in the world? I tell you, the poorest man I know of is the man who has nothing but money, nothing else in the world upon which to devote his ambition and thought. That is the sort of man I consider to be the poorest in the world.

❧

I lived within my means, and my advice to you young men is to do just the same.

❧

I was trained in business affairs, and I was taught how to keep a ledger. The practice of keeping a little personal ledger by young men just starting in business and earning money and requiring to learn its value is, I think, a good one.

It has always been our policy to hear patiently and discuss frankly until the last shred of evidence is on the table, before trying to reach a conclusion and to decide finally upon a course of action.

Now let me leave this little word of counsel for you. Keep a little ledger, as I did. Write down in it what you receive, and do not be ashamed to write down what you pay away. See that you pay it away in such a manner that your father or mother may look over your book and see just what you did with your money. It will help you to save money, and that you ought to do.

When I spoke of the poor man with money I spoke against the poverty of that man who has no affection for anything else, or thought for anything else but money. That kind of man does not help his own character, nor does he build up the character of another.

CHAPTER 4

MONEY AND HAPPINESS

It is wrong to assume that men of immense wealth are always happy.

∞

The penalty of a selfish attempt to make the world confer a living without contributing to the progress or happiness of mankind is generally a failure to the individual. The pity is that when he goes down he inflicts heartache and misery also on others who are in no way responsible.

༄

Do you know the only thing that gives me pleasure? It's to see my dividends coming in.

༄

I was early taught to work as well as play. My life has been one long, happy holiday; full of work and full of play—I dropped the worry on the way—and God was good to me every day.

༄

I can think of nothing less pleasurable than a life devoted to pleasure.

I am sure it is a mistake to assume that the possession of money in great abundance necessarily brings happiness. The very rich are just like all the rest of us; and if they get pleasure from the possession of money, it comes from their ability to do things which give satisfaction to someone besides themselves.

Never lose interest in life and the world. Never allow yourself to become annoyed.

If a man lives his life to himself and has no regard for humanity he will be the most miserable man on Earth. All the money he can get will not help him to forget his discontent. To hide one's self from the world and live alone, secluded from one's fellow men like a hermit, will make a man's nature sullen and wretched.

I believe in the supreme worth of the individual and in his right to life, liberty, and the pursuit of happiness.

The road to happiness lies in two simple principles: find what interests you and that you can do well, and put your whole soul into it—every bit of energy and ambition and natural ability you have.

As I study wealthy men, I can see but one way in which they can secure a real equivalent for money spent, and that is to cultivate a taste for giving where the money may produce an effect which will be a lasting gratification.

⌒◆⌒

I am especially thankful that I learned early to take an interest in other fields than business, so when I was able to shift more and more active business cares from my shoulders to those of other men I could do so without regret for I had other fields of activity awaiting my attention which have proved of absorbing interest.

⌒◆⌒

The only thing which is of lasting benefit to a man is that which he does for himself.

I regard it as of the greatest importance that the man of business should guard against his business monopolizing him to the exclusion of all other fields of life.

What a great boon it is to a man—to have another man tell him that he believes in him, that he trusts him! What a happiness all my business experience has been because my associates believed in me, trusted me implicitly!

CHAPTER 5

RELIGION AND CHARITY

So many people see the pressing needs of everyday life that possibly they fail to realize those which are, if less obvious, of an even larger significance—for instance, the great claims of higher education. Ignorance is the source of a large part of the poverty and a vast amount of the crime in the world—hence the need of education. If we assist the highest forms of education— in whatever field—we secure the widest influence in enlarging the boundaries of human knowledge; for all the new facts discovered or set in motion become the universal heritage.

∽∾

God gave me my money.

∽∾

I believe the power to make money is a gift of God . . . to be developed and used to the best of our ability for the good of mankind. Having been endowed with the gift I possess, I believe it is my duty to make money and still more money and to use the money I make for the good of my fellow man according to the dictates of my conscience.

A large number of individuals are contributing to the support of educational institutions in our country. To help an inefficient, ill-located, unnecessary school is a waste. I am told by those who have given most careful study to this problem that it is highly probable that enough money has been squandered on unwise educational projects to have built up a national system of higher education adequate to our needs if the money had been properly directed to that end.

I believe it is a religious duty to get all the money you can, fairly and honestly; to keep all you can, and to give away all you can.

In this country we have come to the period when we can well afford to ask the ablest men to devote more of their time, thought, and money to the public well-being. I am not so presumptuous as to attempt to define exactly what this betterment work should consist of. Every man will do that for himself, and his own conclusion will be final for himself. It is well, I think, that no narrow or preconceived plan should be set down as the best.

Charity is injurious unless it helps the recipient to become independent of it.

It is easy to do harm in giving money. To give to institutions which should be supported by others is not the best philanthropy. Such giving only serves to dry up the natural springs of charity.

We must always remember that there is not enough money for the work of human uplift and that there never can be. How vitally important it is, therefore, that the expenditure should go as far as possible and be used with the greatest intelligence!

There is nothing in this world that can compare with the Christian fellowship; nothing that can satisfy but Christ.

It is interesting to follow the mental processes that some excellent souls go through to cloud their consciences when they consider what their duty actually is. For instance, one man says: "I do not believe in giving money to street beggars." I agree with him, I do not believe in the practice either; but that is not a reason why one should be exempt from doing something to help the situation represented by the street beggar. Because one does not yield to the importunities of such people is exactly the reason one should join and uphold the charity organization societies of one's own locality, which deal justly and humanely with this class, separating the worthy from the unworthy.

∞

This Sunday school has been of help to me, greater perhaps than any other force in my Christian life, and I can ask no better things for you than that you, and all that shall come after you in this great band of workers for Christ, shall receive the same measure of blessedness which I have been permitted to have.

❦

We frequently make our gifts conditional on the giving of others, not because we wish to force people to do their duty, but because we wish in this way to root the institution in the affections of as many people as possible who, as contributors, become personally concerned, and thereafter may be counted on to give to the institution their watchful interest and cooperation.

❦

We can never learn too much of His will towards us, too much of His messages and His advice. The Bible is His word and its study gives at once the foundation for our faith and an inspiration to battle onward in the fight against the tempter.

After it is all over, the religion of man is his most important possession.

Surely it is wise to be careful not to duplicate effort and not to inaugurate new charities in fields already covered, but rather to strengthen and perfect those already at work. There is a great deal of rivalry and a vast amount of duplication, and one of the most difficult things in giving is to ascertain when the field is fully covered. Many people simply consider whether the institution to which they are giving is thoughtfully and well managed, without stopping to discover whether the field is not already occupied by others; and for this reason one ought not to investigate a single institution by itself, but always in its relation to all similar institutions in the territory.

And we are never too old to study the Bible. Each time the lessons are studied comes some new meaning, some new thought which will make us better.

If the people can be educated to help themselves, we strike at the root of many of the evils of the world. This is the fundamental thing, and it is worth saying even if it has been said so often that its truth is lost sight of in its constant repetition.

Giving should be entered into in just the same way as investing. Giving is investing.

If a combination to do business is effective in saving waste and in getting better results, why is not combination far more important in philanthropic work?

I want to know surely in giving that I am putting money where it will do most good.

I have been frank to say that I believe in the spirit of combination and cooperation when properly and fairly conducted in the world of commercial affairs, on the principle that it helps to reduce waste; and waste is a dissipation of power. I sincerely hope and thoroughly believe that this same principle will eventually prevail in the art of giving as it does in business. It is not merely the tendency of the times developed by more exacting conditions in industry, but it should make its most effective appeal to the hearts of the people who are striving to do the most good to the largest number.

The kind of man I like is one that lives for his fellows—the one that lives in the open, contented with his lot and trying to bestow all the good he can on humanity.

The best philanthropy is constantly in search of the finalities—a search for cause, an attempt to cure evils at their source.

❦

I investigated and worked myself almost to a nervous breakdown, in groping my way through the ever-widening field of philanthropic endeavor.

❦

The whole system of proper relations, whether it be in commerce, or in the Church, or in the sciences, rests on honor. Able business men seek to confine their dealings to people who tell the truth and keep their promises; and the representatives of the Church, who are often prone to attack business men as a type of what is selfish and mean, have some great lessons to learn, and they will gladly learn them as these two types of workers grow closer together.

Go carefully. Be conservative. Be sure you are right, and then do not be afraid to give out, as your heart prompts you, and as the Lord inspires you.

You must put in, if you would take out.

The great value of dealing with an organization which knows all the facts, and can best decide just where the help can be applied to the best advantage, has impressed itself upon me through the results of long years of experience.

It may be asked: How is it consistent with the universal diffusion of these blessings that vast sums of money should be in single hands? The reply is, as I see it, that, while men of wealth control great sums of money, they do not and cannot use them for themselves. They have, indeed, the legal title to large properties, and they do control the investment of them, but that is as far as their own relation to them extends or can be extended. The money is universally diffused, in the sense that it is kept invested and it passes into the pay envelope week by week.

It is the duty of men of means to maintain the title to their property and to administer their funds until some man, or body of men, shall rise up capable of administering for the general good the capital of the country better than they can.

⌘

We cannot afford to have great souls who are capable of doing the most effective work slaving to raise the money. That should be a business man's task, and he should be supreme in managing the machinery of the expenses. The teachers, the workers, and the inspired leaders of the people should be relieved of these pressing and belittling money cares. They have more than enough to do in tilling their tremendous and never fully occupied field, and they should be free from any care which might in any wise divert them from that work.

⌘

If we assist the highest forms of education—in whatever field—we secure the widest influence in enlarging the boundaries of human knowledge.

The best philanthropy, the help that does the most good and the least harm, the help that nourishes civilization at its very root, that most widely disseminates health, righteousness, and happiness, is not what is usually called charity. It is, in my judgment, the investment of effort or time or money, carefully considered with relation to the power of employing people at a remunerative wage, to expand and develop the resources at hand, and to give opportunity for progress and healthful labor where it did not exist before. No mere money-giving is comparable to this in its lasting and beneficial results.

It is a mistake for a man who wishes for happiness and to help others to think that he will wait until he has made a fortune before giving away money to deserving objects.

It is good to know that there are always unselfish men, of the best caliber, to help in every large philanthropic enterprise. One of the most satisfactory and stimulating pieces of good fortune that has come to me is the evidence that so many busy people are willing to turn aside from their work in pressing fields of labor and to give their best thoughts and energies without compensation to the work of human uplift.

CHAPTER 6
ADVICE TO THE NEXT GENERATION

The most important thing for a young man is to establish a credit—a reputation, character.

⚮

The ability to deal with people is as purchasable a commodity as sugar or coffee, and I will pay more for that ability than for any other under the sun.

How many different kinds of friends there are! They should all be held close at any cost; for, although some are better than others, perhaps, a friend of whatever kind is important; and this one learns as one grows older. There is the kind that when you need help has a good reason just at the moment, of course, why it is impossible to extend it.

Try to turn every disaster into an opportunity.

Oftentimes the most difficult competition comes, not from the strong, the intelligent, the conservative competitor, but from the man who is holding on by the eyelids and is ignorant of his costs, and anyway he's got to keep running or bust!

❧

If you want to succeed you should strike out on new paths, rather than travel the worn paths of accepted success.

❧

Study diligently your capital requirements, and fortify yourself fully to cover possible set-backs, because you can absolutely count on meeting setbacks.

❧

Don't be afraid to give up the good to go for the great.

Next to doing the right thing, the most important thing is to let people know you are doing the right thing.

My ideas of business are no doubt old-fashioned, but the fundamental principles do not change from generation to generation, and sometimes I think that our quick-witted American business men, whose spirit and energy are so splendid, do not always sufficiently study the real underlying foundations of business management. I have spoken of the necessity of being frank and honest with oneself about one's own affairs: many people assume that they can get away from the truth by avoiding thinking about it, but the natural law is inevitable, and the sooner it is recognized, the better.

I would rather hire a man with enthusiasm than a man who knows everything.

I believe in the dignity of labor, whether with head or hand; that the world owes no man a living but that it owes every man an opportunity to make a living.

A friendship founded on business is better than a business founded on friendship.

The man who puts up a second factory when the factory in existence will supply the public demand adequately and cheaply is wasting the national wealth and destroying the national prosperity, taking the bread from the laborer and unnecessarily introducing heartache and misery into the world.

Singleness of purpose is one of the chief essentials for success in life, no matter what may be one's aim.

. . . it is worthwhile to emphasize again the fact that it is not merely capital and "plants" and the strictly material things which make up a business, but the character of the men behind these things, their personalities, and their abilities; these are the essentials to be reckoned with.

❧

I believe that thrift is essential to well-ordered living.

❧

I do not think that there is any other quality so essential to success of any kind as the quality of perseverance. It overcomes almost everything, even nature.

❧

The underlying, essential element of success in business affairs is to follow the established laws of high-class dealing. Keep to broad and sure lines, and study them to be certain that they are correct ones.

❧

Do not many of us who fail to achieve big things . . . fail because we lack concentration—the art of concentrating the mind on the thing to be done at the proper time and to the exclusion of everything else?

It has always been my rule in business to make everything count.

The chief advantages from industrial combinations are those which can be derived from a cooperation of persons and aggregation of capital. Much that one man cannot do alone two can do together, and once admit the fact that cooperation, or, what is the same thing, combination, is necessary on a small scale, the limit depends solely upon the necessities of business.

I should say in general the advantage of education is to better fit a man for life's work. I would advise young men to take a college course, as a rule, but think some are just as well off with a thorough business training.

It is very important to remember what other people tell you, not so much what you yourself already know.

Success comes from keeping the ears open and the mouth closed.

If you aim for a large, broad-gauged success, do not begin your business career, whether you sell your labor or are an independent producer, with the idea of getting from the world by hook or crook all you can. In the choice of your profession or your business employment, let your first thought be: Where can I fit in so that I may be most effective in the work of the world? Where can I lend a hand in a way most effectively to advance the general interests?

Save when you can and not when you have to.

When we look around us and see the continual progress education is making, and also the great changes which have been constantly taking place since it began to rise, we cannot but think everyone ought to endeavor to improve the great opportunities which are now offered them. Had Isaac Newton been an unlearned man, on seeing the apple fall to the ground, would he not rather have eaten it than inquired why it fell?

∞

A laborer is worthy of his hire, no less, but no more, and in the long run he must contribute an equivalent for what he is paid. If he does not do this, he is probably pauperized, and you at once throw out the balance of things. You can't hold up conditions artificially, and you can't change the underlying laws of trade. If you try, you must inevitably fail. All this may be trite and obvious, but it is remarkable how many men overlook what should be the obvious. These are facts we can't get away from—a business man must adapt himself to the natural conditions as they exist from month to month and year to year.

❧

I didn't think of discouragement. What I thought of was getting that job. I simply had to get work, for father said if I could not find anything to do I might go back to the country.

❧

I believe the only way to succeed is to keep getting ahead all the time.

❧

Don't even think of temporary or sharp advantages. Don't waste your effort on a thing which ends in a petty triumph unless you are satisfied with a life of petty success. Be sure that before you go into an enterprise you see your way clear to stay through to a successful end. Look ahead.

Don't be a good fellow. I love my fellow man and I take great interest in him. But don't be convivial, always ready to pitch in and be one of the crowd. Be moderate. Be very moderate. Don't let good fellowship get the least hold on you. If you do, you are lost, not only you but your progeny, your family for generations to come.

I admire persistence. It is commendable, especially in young men, and it will win in the end.

The person who starts out simply with the idea of getting rich won't succeed; you must have a larger ambition. There is no mystery in business success. If you do each day's task successfully, and stay faithfully within these natural operations of commercial laws which I talk so much about, and keep your head clear, you will come out all right.

❦

Do not be discouraged . . . I had many refusals, I did not give up.

❦

I was taught to be self-reliant.

❦

I could not have done for myself better than I did for my employer. How I wish all young men could know that the way to hold a position is to do just that thing! You who employ young men know that some young men expect to do just as little as they can and are much troubled all the time that they do not get an increase in salary. That doesn't make a very permanent relationship with some business men— they look for some other to fill the place.

Be sure that you are not deceiving yourself at any time about actual conditions. The man who starts out simply with the idea of getting rich won't succeed; you must have a larger ambition.

They are in the embarrassing position that their fathers have great sums of money, and those boys have not a ghost of a chance to compete with you who come from the country and who want to do something in the world. You are in training now to shortly take the places of those young men. I suppose you cannot realize how many eyes are upon you and how great is the increasing interest that is taken in you. You may not think that, when you are lonely and find it difficult to get a footing. But it is true that, in a place like this, true interest is taken in you. When I left the school house I came into a place similar to this, where I associated with people whom it was good to know. Nothing better could have happened to me.

∽

I would name as another help in this same direction the fact that from my earliest recollection I had a peculiar training in my home. It seemed to be a business training from the very beginning. I was taught to do things, simple things such as a boy could do. I was taught to be self-reliant. At the age of seven or eight I was taught, as a boy in the country, to milk a cow. I could milk a cow as well as a man could. That is a very simple thing to refer to, but that was one of the things I began to learn. I was taught at the age of eight to drive a horse, and to drive him just as carefully as a man could. I remember very well the instruction of my father: "My son, hold very carefully going down the hill. Don't let him stumble. When you are on the level road, let him trot right along." And I never shall forget that.

CHAPTER 7

JOHN D. ROCKEFELLER'S PERSONAL CORRESPONDENCE

❦ ❦

CORRESPONDENCE WITH HIS SON, JOHN D.
ROCKEFELLER, JR.

New York
November 28th, 1887

Dear John:
    Yours, of the 22nd, duly received.
Excuse delay in answering. Have also your
telegram of today for the cutter, and will
attend to it tomorrow morning. I assume

you want the one to carry two persons. I had a pleasant time in Washington. It is a beautiful city. The weather was mild and lovely. After receiving my testimony they did not wish any other although they had subpoenaed eight of us. We feel very well about the experience over there. The New York World hasn't any further ammunition in this direction, is now going back to its first love, the Buffalo suit, trying to rake up something against us. Had a delightful Sunday at home yesterday. Feeling well and ready for business. Looking forward with pleasure to seeing you the last of this week.

Concur in your decision about painting the storm doors. You and Mother will surely have your own way in all these affairs, what's the use of my saying a word. You are monarch of all you survey.

Your loving Father

New York
January 20th, 1888

My Dear Son:

We all welcomed yours of the 15th. We're very pleased to hear of your daily experience, and hope both you and Mother will be much better for this quiet country life. I am glad you know about it. It carries me back to my boyhood days. I am having a pair of shoes made to lace up. I am told they support the ankles better. I will bring them with me. Please tell Mother that everything is being done that can be in reference to the telephone wire to Forest Hill. A new route is desired and the effort to secure it makes a little delay. Aunty and I went to the Harlem River this morning with Flash and Midnight in a new cutter which cost $300. Very extravagant, I know, but the sleighing is so good could not resist the temptation to buy it and hope to get the worth of our money. I drove four times day before yesterday and three times yesterday making an aggregate in the two days of about 80 miles. Don't you think I am an enthusiastic youth? I am looking forward with great pleasure to seeing you next week but may not leave until Friday.

Lovingly,
Your Father

∞

New York
January 26, 1895

My Dear Son:

I enclose check to your order for twenty-one dollars, for your twenty-first birthday, being one for each year.

It would be very pleasant if we could all spend the day together at home, but I think under the circumstances, it is better for you to remain at college as you have been obliged to be away from your work so much of late.

I cannot tell you how much happiness we all have in you. And how much we are looking forward to, and relying on you for in the future.

We are grateful beyond measure for your promise and for the confidence your life inspires in us, not only, but in all your friends and acquaintances and this is of more value than all earthly possessions.

We all join in the hope that this and all the days to come may bring only good to you, and we rejoice that you know from experience, that good for you is inseparably connected with the good you bring to others. But this is not a lecture, only a kind word from an affectionate father to a much loved and only son on the occasion of his twenty-first birthday.

John D. Rockefeller

Providence, R.I.
February 3, 1895

Dear Father,

I want again to thank you for the check which you sent me last week and also for the letter that accompanied it.

I am grateful if my life brings happiness to you; it should bring much more than I have made it. But had I done infinitely better than I have in this particular, I should not even then have made anything like an adequate return for all that you have done for me.

I am glad for the confidence which you say my life inspires in you. I feel that I have but too little confidence in myself; but the very fact of you having faith in me will help me to make the most of my life.

Be assured, dear Father, that my greatest happiness will ever be to do my utmost for you and Mother, and not only to keep clean, but be a credit to the honorable and noble record which you have made. People talk about sons being better than their fathers, but if I can be half as generous, half as unselfish, and half as kindly affectionate to my fellow men as you have been, I shall not feel that my life has been in vain.

Affectionately,
John

New York
November 11, 1899

Dear Father

I want to tell you again of my very deep appreciation of the generous, patient, and kindly way in which you have treated me during the anxiety and pressure which has been brought upon you this week largely through me. Most Fathers would have upbraided and stormed, and that too, justly. Because of your forbearance and gentleness you have caused me to feel more deeply the lesson which this has taught. I would rather have had my right hand cut off than to have caused you this anxiety. My one thought and purpose since I came into the office has been to relieve you in every way possible of the burdens which you have carried so long. To realize now that instead of doing that I have been partially and largely instrumental in adding to your burdens, is bitter and humiliating. My effort has been an honest one although I have failed in its accomplishment. I want fully to acknowledge my mistake and to shoulder the blame which rightfully belongs to me. With your expression of continued confidence which I most truly appreciate, I shall try again in the hope that I can live my appreciation of your magnanimity far better than I can express it in words. This has been a hard lesson but it may help me to avoid harder ones in the future.

Affectionately,
John

Augusta, Georgia
January 18, 1909

Dear Son:

I thank you a thousand times for the fur coat and cap and mittens. I did not feel that I could afford such luxuries, and am grateful for a son who is able to buy them for me. Be assured that they are much appreciated. Mother unites with me in thanking you.

Affectionately,
Father

New York
January 11, 1910

Dear Father:

Since you have upon previous occasions expressed an interest in the total amount of money which I spend in a year you will be interested to know that my total expenditures for the year 1909 is $86,288.35. Subtracting from this amount $25,000 which I gave to Brown, leaves a total of $58,238.35. The total last year was $65,918.47. This excess in 1908 is accounted for by the amount which I gave away during that year as compared with the amount given away in 1909 less the $25,000 above referred to.

Affectionately,
John

Lakewood, NJ
May 9, 1917

Dear Son:

A brief word only! History is making so rapidly, I can hardly keep up with it, but this fact is being very forcibly impressed upon my mind that my individual ability to do things for others is only a fraction of what it was before the government took a first mortgage on my possessions and my income, requiring me to pay for governmental purposes many millions of dollars each year. With this in view, we must all reflect very carefully before any further committals are made for gifts of money, especially as I can now see where I shall require to pay in a very few months no less than twenty millions of dollars, not including what I have already paid and for which I am already in debt.

All goes well with us, and we are happy and contented and hope that you and Abby will be rational, restful, retiring, and right minded, and you will look with righteous indignation upon any overtaxing of your time and strength, remembering that you have much work to do in the world and it cannot all be done in a day. Be patient and be moderate. Allow other people to bear some of their share of the burdens of life, and in the end you will accomplish more, live longer, and be happier.

Affectionately,
Father

Lakewood, NJ
July 30, 1918

Dear Son:

I am this day giving you 18,800 shares of the common stock of the American Linseed Company and 22,400 shares of the preferred, and 500 shares of the Lakewood Engineering Company, 4,200 shares of the International Agricultural Corporation Preferred, 12,423 shares of the Atlantic Refining Company, 37,269 shares of the Vacuum Oil Company, and 13,000 shares of the Standard Oil Company of New Jersey, and I have requested Mr. Houston to have the same transferred to you.

Affectionately,
Father

New York
February 11, 1919

Dear Father:

Once more my breath is taken by the receipt of your letter of February 5th announcing the stupendous gift of New Jersey stock which you are making to me. I need not tell you how deeply I realize the great responsibility which each of these gifts bring, for every day of my life I realize more fully the peculiar obligations which rest upon those of large means. A sense of the burden of the responsibility which, through your great generosity has come so rapidly to me during the passing years, would be almost crushing were it not off-set by the vision of the wonderful opportunity for useful service which comes with responsibility.

I appreciate more and more each day what your wisdom and intelligence

and broad vision in giving has meant
to the world. I realize increasingly the
tremendous value that attaches to your
endorsement of an enterprise, business
or philanthropic, and I need not assure
you that it will be my great pride, as well
as my solemn duty, to endeavor, while
emulating your unparalleled generosity, to
live up to the high standards of intelligent
giving which you have set. Whenever I
am discouraged because of the littleness
and the meanness and the petty jealousy
of men, I find renewed courage as I
contemplate your patience, your bigness of
heart, your Christian tolerance. Whenever
I am oppressed with the feeling that
one man can do so little even when he is
doing his utmost, I only have to review
the marvelous accomplishments of your
extraordinary life in order to be heartened
for the task which lies before me.

May the God who has led you so
wonderfully during all these years of your
life, Whom you have served so faithfully

and so untiringly, lead me in the same path of duty and of service, and help me to carry on worthily the works for mankind which with marvelous prevision you have so solidly and wisely established.

I thank you, dear Father, for this great gift, and for the continued confidence in me which it implies. May God bless you and help me to live up to the high ideals which have guided your life.

Lovingly,
John

New York
October 22, 1920

Dear Son:

I am giving you a check for $500,000. It will be available for use on Monday next.

Affectionately,
Father

New York
October 23, 1920

Dear Son:
 I am giving you a check for $500,000. It will be available for use on Tuesday next.
 Affectionately,
 Father

New York
October 28, 1920

Dear Son:
 I am today giving you a check for $500,000. It will be available for use at once.
 Affectionately,
 Father

❧❧

New York
October 28, 1920

Dear Father:

What a delightful habit you are forming! This third gift, of which your letter of October 28th advises me, is as acceptable as was the first.

Again I would express my truest thanks. How can I ever make clear to you how much I appreciate your wonderful generosity!

Affectionately,
John

❧❧

Florida
January 26, 1922

Dear Son:

As to the sums which I have handed you from time to time, it is to be remembered that I have already set aside large amounts in our different trusts, for benevolent purposes, in addition to my regular giving personally, and with the careful and protracted study which I give to each object of any considerable moment, it is evident that I shall not fulfill to the complete extent, my heart's desire to make everything that I can give to the world available, for many years to come.

As you are in touch with the world from a somewhat different angle from mine, and there have been ample means left by a kind Providence. I have hoped that with your constant and careful studies, and wide and broad knowledge of the needs of the world, you would have the fullest enjoyment in personally determining and carrying out plans of your own for helping the world, and I rejoice to afford you this opportunity, in the confident assurance that great good will result therefrom.

I am indeed blessed beyond measure in having a son whom I can trust to do this

most particular and most important work.
Go carefully. Be conservative. Be sure you
are right—and then do not be afraid to
give out, as your heart prompts you, and as
the Lord inspires you.

With tenderest affection,
Father

Hôtel Baur au Lac Zurich
September 4, 1915

Dear Father:

I want to thank you for your birthday cheque which is always welcome.

My thoughts in regard to the early history of yours and Mother's lives together is only for family research. It is the link in our family history which you alone can give now to hand down to your children, as I will hand down to my children dates and events in Harold's and my early lives together. Mother used to tell us about your going to school, about how you were dressed the first time you called, about your wedding and the early days in Cheshire Street. I am sure that you understand what I mean.

We would all like to help in your philanthropies. It is beautiful and developing work and John is privileged in a way which Alta and I as yet have not had the opportunity of being. I am sure that as women we are serious minded and earnest and deeply interested in mankind and that we would only be too glad to shoulder our inherited responsibilities if we were permitted to.

Fowler expects to sail back to school in a few days. We have had a beautiful summer all together.

May each day bring some new beauty into your life, dear Father, and may you feel the love of your children near you.

With repeated thanks and my love.

Your loving daughter,

Edith

Hôtel Bar au Lac Zurich
October 22, 1915

Dear Father:

Your cheque on the anniversary of
Mother's birth linked together the past
and the present and showed me that you
still hold me in your remembrance. There
is warmth and love in your heart when one
can get through all the outside barriers
which you have thrown up to protect
yourself—your own self—from the world.
This warmth and love draws me, for is it
not living?

Thank you,
Father.
Affectionately,
Edith

Hôtel Bar au Lac Zurich
January 31, 1916

Dear Father:

I want to thank you for your Christmas cheque which brings with it to me your thought and remembrance.

Also, I want to ask you if you will give me some more stocks in order to increase my income. In 1908 you gave me some S.O. stocks ($10,000.00), in 1909 or 1910 you gave me the Riverside property, and since then my principal and my allowance have remained the same. For myself I spend a sixth or seventh of my allowance and the rest I give away. As a woman of 43 I would like to have more money to help with. There are causes in which I am interested which are uplifting and of vital importance to my development which I cannot help as I should like to because I have not the money. I hope you will see that as a woman of earnestness of purpose and singleness of spirit I am worthy of more confidence on your part.

Hoping that you have entirely recovered from your cold, and with renewed thanks and love.

Affectionately,
Edith

⸎

Hôtel Bar au Lac Zurich
June 22, 1917

Dear Father:
We are thinking of your birthday which is approaching and are happy in the thought that you are well and happy. I wish some times that you would let me get nearer to you—your real self, so that your heart would feel the warmth of a simple human soul. Perhaps you will let me some day.

For this coming year on which you are just entering I wish you continued health and joy, and I send to you many loving wishes.

Your affectionate daughter,

Edith

P.S. For all the help which you are giving in so many times I am grateful and appreciative. Edith

⧡

July 27, 1917

Dear Daughter:

I thank you for your beautiful letter on the occasion of my 78th birthday. I can think of nothing which I would more devoutly desire than that we should be constantly drawn closer and closer together, to the end that we may be of the greatest assistance to each other, not only, but to the dear ones so near and so dear to us.

All goes well with us at Forest Hill. It was never so beautiful here before. Our thoughts go out to all the dear ones, the memory of whom makes the place so sweet and sacred to me.

With tenderest love for each and every one of you, I am,

Affectionately,
Father

∞

April 9, 1921

Dear Edith:

Answering yours of the 10th ult., I cherish no unkindly feelings, but I could not say I did not regret you should not have taken my advice in respect to the use of the funds which I had given you.

However, while we have all suffered in this connection, for such things cannot be hid under a bushel, as perhaps I intimated in some former letter, yet you have had to bear most, and now, as to the future of your financial management I see no other way than that you will have to cut your garment to suit the cloth.

But, Edith dear, the financial question, while important, is not important when compared to the other question—the great question of your being present with your children. And how sadly they need your presence, and how very solicitous we all are for them! In this connection I may add that you could have been a great comfort and help to your mother and me. But this sinks into insignificance also, when we consider the dear children, and the importance of the constant, jealous, watch-care of the mother, and the untold sorrow that may be entailed upon us all. Edith dear, you know it all, and so much better than I—indeed, I know so little. The responsibility is with you. I hope it is not too late.

This knowledge adds to my burdens, and with increasing years, though I do not complain, I have enough, possibly more than I should undertake to carry.

I am not lecturing. I am not scolding. I love you, Edith dear; and I am still hoping.

Affectionately,
Father

Chicago, IL
September 9, 1922

Dear Father:

Today is dear Mother's birthday, and as my thoughts turn to her in loving remembrance I am impelled to send you just a word of love.

One of my earliest remembrances is being wakened in the city house in Cleveland by your voice as you talked to Mother from your bathroom where you were dressing, while she coiffed her hair in your bedroom. Alta and I slept in the room next to your bathroom, and your voice which was deep and full, came through to us as you talked on. Then I remember sitting on Mother's lap by the middle front window in the music room, while she cut my nails (I must have been very young). Then I remember your sitting in front of the fire in the music room after luncheon on Sunday, and taking the meat out of a hickory nut for me with a nut picker. And then, one morning while Mother was playing the piano, you came up and rubbed my back which was making me restless on account of the prickly heat. You came up so quietly and you went down again so quietly. These are some of my earliest remembrances.

Mother's love for children and her belief that to mould them was building for the future was an inspiration in her life, perhaps even the greatest one.

It is nice to be together again for a while as we were for so many years—you, Mother, and I. She lives with us still, and her good works follow her.

As ever, Your loving daughter,
Edith

LETTERS TO JOHN D. ROCKEFELLER

Mr. Rockefeller
Cleveland, Ohio

Dear Sir,

You may consider this rather a strange letter coming from a stranger as it does, one whom you never met.

I am not quite forty years of age, was a soldier in the late war, where I was when I should have been at school, studying a profession, or learning a trade, and while in the service of my country I was taken prisoner and was confined at Andersonville and other prisons for about 10 months, the history of which is known to everyone, I might better explain my case by quoting from a letter I wrote to Genl. Lagan in 74 in an appeal to Congress, "There are today thousands of men whose constitutions are broken down and are not the same and never will be the same, men who are apparently well, yet whose systems are entirely wrong, who are young in years yet have all the symptoms of old men whose race is about run. Let every man put himself in his (the Prisoner's) place, turned into a pen like cattle with no shelter, nothing to protect one from the storm's blast, or the heat of the sun, filth and vermin surrounding him on every side, starvation staring him in the face day after day, week after week, and month after month, what would compensate you for such a life as this, yet thousands did it," and I was one of them barefooted, shirtless, through winter storms, sickness, no Doctor, no kind nurse, no bed but hard mother earth, such sir was a part of my lot, and today I am feeling the effects of these fearful months of starvation.

I have struggled along to try to get a little ahead, but have failed. I have taken an active part in politics in hopes of getting some lucrative position by which I could keep myself and family, but have been unsuccessful, and so I thought I would write this letter to you, knowing that you had enough and to spare. I felt that it would do no harm to ask even if I did not succeed, for if one does not ask how does one know his needs, for it is written "ask and yea shall receive," "seek and yea shall find," "knock and it shall be opened unto you." I don't know why I wrote the above quotations for I am not a professor, but they came into my head and I wrote them, I am poor but have so much desired to get something ahead so that I might open a small suburb grocery store where I might hold my own and make enough to live on, and for this reason I write to you hoping that you might be able to help me poor Andersonville boy . . .

Yours Respectfully,
John R. Campbell

∽∞∾

Long Island City
Mr. J. D. Rockefeller

Dear Sir,

It is with a feeling of misgiving and diffidence with which I address this note to you; and it is only my great anxiety for the cause I present, which prompts me for the first time in my life to "beg" from a total stranger.

I know that a gentleman in your position is approached from every side to aid religious and charitable objects, but I do hope you will take this subject into consideration and give a favorable answer to my request. The enclosed card will speak for itself. There have been three hundred of these cards issued, thirty of which I hold. It is about all our church can do by great effort to keep up or current expenses which amount to about $4,000.

Our building is very much out of repair! It is absolutely necessary to raise it and put it in an upright position; repair the roof and numerous other things which amount to about $2,500.

Our pastor Mr. Randall brought the subject before the Long Island Baptist Association and that body recommended him to the Brooklyn churches to solicit aid from them, provided we would liquidate our debt. That is impossible for us to do alone. The members are none of them in flourishing circumstances, but have done nobly this far. Now would you please interest yourself in us. Make inquiries and you will find all I write and more is true of our struggle. If you could only interest the large company (which has made so much of its money right in this place) to give a very little of their abundance, it would be a Godsend to the Each One Baptist Church of Long Island City.

With many apologies for my intrusion and sincere hopes that my effort will be fruitful of some acknowledgment,

I remain very respectfully,

Clara F. Burnett

Richmond, VA
Mr. Rockefeller

Dear Sir,

Having seen from our papers that you are a Baptist (and a very liberal one) I am prompted to ask your aid in building Grove Ave Church. It is being erected in a growing part of this city where our denomination is greatly in need of a good commodious house of worship.

The congregation is too small and poor to complete it without help. Will you not kindly aid us in this arduous undertaking! Whatever you may be willing to give, will be gratefully received and promptly acknowledged. I enclose a clip cut from the paper . . .

Should you favor me with a donation, please address

Mrs. S. L. Burress
Of Baltimore U.O.C.
Richmond, VA

Mr. J. D. Rockefeller

Kind Sir,

Knowing that you are a gentleman of means and being in very straitened circumstances I take the liberty of asking a favor of you. I wish to know if you would loan me some money as I have a heavy mortgage on my furniture on which I have to pay a heavy interest—and can-not pay the principal that is why I ask this favor of you. I will secure you by giving you a mortgage and pay you a fair interest on your money. I am a lone woman keeping boarders for my living. The amount I wish to borrow is three hundred dollars. If you wish to accommodate me please answer by the bearer or in person.

Very Respectfully yours,
Mrs. M. Camp

Cleveland, OH
September 16, 1890

Mr. Rockefeller,

Would you like to buy a farm on the Lake Shore? I have a farm of about seventy acres. It has a large frontage on the lake. It is a valuable piece of property and I would not part with it if it was possible to keep it. It is a place my husband bought before going into the army. I have been obliged to get quite a heavy mortgage on it. My health is very poor so my expenses are greater.

Hearing of your kindness to others I thought I would write and ask you if you would buy my place. It is hardly a mile below Point Breeze.

Please let me know and oblige.

Mrs. G. P. Gunn

❦

Mr. Rockefeller

Dear Sir,

Reading from time to time, in the papers, of your immense wealth, and of the much good you are doing in the world, I have been led to enquire, if it is possible you are a cousin of mine. I will tell you who I am and perhaps you may recall the facts to memory. I am Harry Avery's youngest daughter, my name is Helen, and will be fifty-one years old, the twenty-seventh of this month. I well remember my dear aunt Lucy Rockefeller, about twenty-five years ago. I went to Marathon to visit her—she was living then with her son in law Abraham Borz. I also visited to Egbert Rockefellers. A few years later my Mother died and Aunt Lucy came and kept house for father nearly a year. I was married and living at that time on a farm adjoining father's. I remember William Rockefeller, his wife and two children that visited us when we lived there. After years of toil to pay for the small farm we had bought, we moved to Cayuga Co. and having sold that one bought another one here, a larger one, and had the times been as good as when we came here we should have been all right. But (Mr. Bush) my husband's health failed him and he has not been able to labor any to speak of since. We have five children. They are all married except our youngest boy. He is fifteen years old and we are trying as best we can to educate him. In order to do this we thought we would let our elder son carry on the farm, and we came to Auburn where we now live thinking to get cheap rent and save paying his board. This we could not do, for circumstances would not admit. We have been here a year, paid twelve dollars and a half per month rent, and find we cannot—with close economy—keep him in school. He is a lovely boy and—having a bad habit—a member of the M. E. Church and we hope to make a man of influence of him, the Lord helping us.

He will go and work through the vacation to help clothe himself. I never thought I would beg, but I am going to ask you to lend a helping hand if you should prove to be my relative, that I may see him educated. We have an indebtedness of two thousand dollars to pay, which keeps our means limited, and only a small rent coming from the farm. I am sure God will reward you and we shall be ever grateful.

Respectfully Yours,
Mrs. Helen E. Bush

Baylor University
Mr. John D. Rockefeller

Dear Sir,

I have no doubt you get so many letters similar to this, that you throw them away—but I have prayed earnestly to God that he will incline you to read this letter from a Texas Baptist Sister. I presume you have heard of Dr. R. C. Burleson (my husband) who has been struggling for the last forty years to build up a great Texas Baptist University. And I am happy to say he has at last succeeded. Baylor University has today the best buildings & campus in the South. Employs 26 Profs & teachers & enrolled last year 687 students and expects to enroll 800 this year. But our money & means are inadequate. We greatly need some finishing touches. We need a dining room. At present we eat in the hall, which is very much crowded & very dark. I succeeded so well in getting two parlors, two society rooms and one library room nicely furnished that I tell our friends that I don't intend to stop till I get our front Parlor elegantly furnished & a dining room built. This is our situation & the object of this letter is to ask you to supply us with means sufficient to build our two story dining room (the upper story to be used for a study hall). Our agents are trying to raise the money & it will probably be raised but I am so anxious to have it completed in our day. When we were at the National Educational Ass. this summer we expected to visit you at your home in Cleveland but learned you were in N.Y. I am sure if we could have seen you & presented our wants in person, you could have better understood our needs. I hope you won't think it bold in thus addressing you, but when I read in the papers of your wonderful gifts & hearing of your great wealth & greater liberality must be my apology. I suppose one of your wealth is so often accustomed to letters of this kind that you will not take time to read half you receive—but be this as it may. I have a little faith that you will at least read this letter as it comes from Texas.

We want to see all these buildings handsomely furnished & out of debt & then we want to retire & spend our last days in quiet & rest. I was very anxious to write this letter to you when we were in Chicago this summer & get Mr. Chambers & Rev. P. G. Henson to help me & endorse it—but put it off. After wishing you great success & begging pardon for thus addressing you—with the hope & earnest prayer that you will consider this request with a favorable response—will close.

Most Respectfully,
Mrs. R.C. Burleson

❧

John D. Rockefeller

My Dear Sir:
This appeal is sent you because, 1st You have the money and we have not; 2nd

It is a worthy cause; 3rd You are a Baptist and interested in the spread of Baptist principles.

Silk business is poor in Paterson. There have been several failures and strikes. If we can get help now our future is assured. The Lord is in this and we will win. My people have given all they can. I am trying to raise $1,000. Have $200 of it. Will you assist? I enclose stamp for your answer and return of the testimonial of Bro. Hon. If desirable I can call on you at your convenience, for explanation. A check to my order will be duly acknowledged.

Respectfully,
A. M. Hand pastor (4th Church)